THREADS
OF
LIFE
Stitched in Rhyme

By Sandra Parr Stonecipher

Threads of Life
Stitched In Rhyme
By: Sandra Parr Stonecipher

Copyright 2003
First Printing

Original Art Work by John Haney

Printed in the USA by
ADR BookPrint
2012 Northern
Wichita, KS 67216

Dedication

For my children: Deanna and Jim Young, Julie and Randy Wilson, and Jeff and Sharen Parr. Also, my grandchildren, Jason and Katie Young, Justin and Annie Young, Audra and Kara Wilson, and my husband, Stoney. What a blessing all of you have been to my life.

ACKNOWLEDGEMENT

I want to thank my friend Virginia Redshaw Wheelhouse for being my biggest cheerleader since I started writing poems many years ago. She has always encouraged me to write this book, especially when I doubted. She is a loving, caring person, and I am proud to call her my friend. I have included a poem I wrote for her on her 81st birthday, "Yes, Santa Claus, There is a Virginia." She is now 87 and still going strong.

I want to thank my husband, Stoney, for all the computer help and moral support, and also for his work designing the cover. I could never have done this without him.

A big thank you to John Haney for doing such a great (and quick) job on the art work.

I'd like to thank my grandson Jason Young for editing this book. He worked really hard, and made many changes that I changed back, so it is not his fault that I insist on using bad grammar. I just like the sounds and rhythm of words that, perhaps, are not proper English.

And thanks to my sister Thelma Taylor and daughter Deanna Young for their thoughts and ideas for the title and cover.

Preface

I cannot say writing this book was a life long dream. In fact, I do not actually know or understand how it all came about. I have only written for the past twenty years or so. I wrote a thought one day into a poem. More thoughts came and so did more poems. I wrote one for my grandson Jason's 18th birthday and also wrote poems for my daughters. After a few years, I realized I had enough poems to make a book. At that point I was only interested in doing one for my family, but decided that I wanted to share with others. I started talking about publishing, but that was as far as I went. After several years of writing, I bought a computer.

I thought all I had to do was type my poems. I was certainly wrong about that. This has been many hours of work. Well, the computer wouldn't do my book for me, but then I met Stoney on the Web chat program ICQ. We have been married for four years this July. I say we are lucky. He says we're blessed. He said he would help me with my book once we were married, but we started remodeling, bowling, and other things. This May, something inspired me to start writing again. In less than a month, I wrote about half the poems in this book, typed them into the computer, contacted publishers and an artist, and formatted the book.

Everyone tells me I have a gift. I do believe that, as many of the poems seem to be just waiting for me to write them down. I believe God gives us all gifts, but using them can be difficult.

I have written everything in plain and simple language so that anyone can enjoy and understand what is being said. Some poems include explanatory notes about where or how I got inspired to write them. I think you will be able to see yourself or others in many of the poems. I hope you enjoy reading them.

Sandra Parr Stonecipher

TABLE OF CONTENTS

CHAPTER 3: WAR AND RELIGION

CHAPTER 4: THE "LITE" SIDE OF DIETING

CHAPTER 5: HUMOR

CHAPTER
I
PEOPLE

I wrote this for my daughters, Julia Ann Wilson and Deanna Elyse Young. I am very proud of them and proud to be their mother.

My Little Girl

God sat down in his workshop
One warm and sunny day
And began to make a baby girl
From a tiny piece of clay.

The skin was creamy, smooth, and soft.
The cheeks a rosy red.
A wisp of hair, with little curls,
Was placed upon the head.

For the heart, He picked the biggest one,
Then into it He bestowed
Patience, kindness, caring, love...
So much it overflowed.

The eyes were shined and polished;
He made them big and blue.
Then He breathed in her the breath of life,
As only God can do.

When He was finished with the job,
Heaven's choir began to sing,
As she was sent to live on earth
On the tip of an angel's wing.

From a tiny babe, to a little girl.
Into a woman, she has grown.
Any mother would be very proud
To call this child her own.

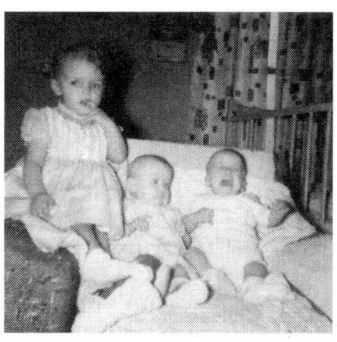

Deanna,
Julie and her twin brother Jeff

Yes, Santa Claus, There is a Virginia

Yes, my dear old Santa Claus,
There's a Virginia, and we know
That though she's turning eighty-one,
She's always on the go.

She can get up in the morning,
Before the rising sun.
When other folks are getting up,
She's got a day's work done.

She's a mother, daughter, sister, wife,
Grandmother...a great one, too.
You cannot count her many friends
Or the things that she can do.

Virginia went to Western
To study there to teach.
She goes to church and Sunday school,
And practices what THEY preach.

Her heart's as young as a newborn babe.
As big as the open sky.
Softer than a feather pillow
Or clouds just floating by.

Thanksgiving is her birthday,
So I'm writing this to show
How thankful that our paths have crossed,
Because I admire and love her so.

Happy Birthday to a grand lady
From your friend, Sandra

*I wrote this poem for my friend Virginia Wheelhouse Red-
shaw on her 81st birthday. She is now a young 87. She's
shown here on May 23, 2003, holding a doily I gave her.*

Mamma Says

Every time we got ready
To go anywhere,
Mama would worry
About our underwear.
"Does it have any holes?
Oh, if it were seen,
I'd be so embarrassed
If it wasn't clean.
If someone got sick,
Or we had a wreck...
Oh, by the way,
Let me check your neck."
When we took a bath,
One of her biggest fears
Was our getting out
Without washing our ears.
She'd spit on her hanky
While eyeballing us.
She'd rub at our face.
We'd yell and we'd fuss.
"Did you wash your face?"
"Did you comb your hair?"
"Please pull up your stocking."
"Sit straight in that chair."

"Don't play in the rain.
I don't want you sick."
"Get out of my flower bed,
And throw down that stick."
"Don't run with sharp objects.
Don't jump on the bed."
Over and over
These cautions were said.
"Were you born in a barn?"
I said, "Shut the door!"
"Please pick up your clothes
From off of the floor."

"Eat all of your carrots.
They're good for your eyes."
"You know where you'll go
If you tell any lies."
"Your eyes will freeze
If you cross them again."
"Please pick up your napkin,
And wipe off your chin."
"Don't swallow those seeds.
In your stomach they'll grow.
How many times
Have I told you so?"

"Take that out of your mouth!
Do you know where it's been?"
To disobey orders
To her was a sin.
At times we were threatened
By her counting to three.
Said, "We'll cross that bridge
When the bridge we can see."
"I'm not telling you this
Just to hear my head rattle.
When your father gets home
I'll let him use the paddle."

"Don't sing at the table."
"Don't talk when you chew."
All these and more
We just couldn't do.
"Like mother, like daughter"
It's repeated again,
For I've said all these things
Like Mama, back then.

The idea for the next poem came from my friend and co-worker, Sandy Chockley. I was probably reading her one of my latest poems when she said, "Why don't you write about Grandma's apron. You could write all of the things that she used it for." Both of my grandmas and my mother wore aprons all the time. They had older ones for everyday use and nicer ones for company and Sundays. Also, they always wore cotton stockings with garters right under their knees. It is a bit different from the looks of grandmothers of today. They look, dress, and act more like their grandchildren. Sometimes I am saddened by the changing times, but I'm glad clothing styles have changed.

Grandma's Apron

When my mind goes reaching back in time,
A precious memory I recall
Is my grandma and her apron,
It's my favorite one of all.

She'd stand in front of her old cook stove,
Beads of sweat upon her brow.
She'd dab at them with her apron.
In my mind I see her now.

When someone came to visit
And knocked upon the door,
She'd reach to dry her hands upon
The apron that she wore.

Her apron would be white with flour
Whenever she would bake.
Throughout the town and neighborhood
All her goodies she would take.

Sometimes we'd just go walking
Through the woods, on a sunny day.
The apron would be full of things
We'd picked along the way.

When I was hurt or feeling sad
During all my growing years,
The apron was the thing she used
To wipe away my tears.

I seldom saw my grandma
Without her little apron on.
So when they came to tell me
My dear grandma was gone,

I knew that they had dressed her
In her finest Sunday best.
But the apron was the final touch
When they laid grandma to rest.

*The apron was the thing
she used to wipe away my
tears.*

11

I wrote this poem about Dr. Dohner a few years ago, and it was published in the Rushville Times. It only mentions a few of the things that Dr. Dohner does for the people of Rushville. He is at his office and the hospital every day, and his price is still only $5.00. After the poem appeared in the newspaper, many called or told me in person, "That is just what I wanted to say about him, but didn't know how to do it." It is an honor to know Dr. Dohner and his sister Clarice, who worked in his office for more than 40 years.

Photo: Courtesy of The Rushville Times

Our Doctor Dohner

God began to shape and mold the clay,
Then said with a tender smile,
"This is a special piece you know,
I've been saving it for awhile.
I've been looking down upon the Earth,
And there's lots of sickness there.
So I'm going to make this special man
And put them in his care."

Then He filled the head with the knowledge
That was needed for His plans.
A kind and caring heart He made,
And skill was placed upon the hands.
He blessed a place called Rushville
When He sent him to that town.
The sick would come to him for help
From miles and miles around.
Some were wealthy, some so poor
They didn't have a dime,
But it never mattered to that man,
He gave them equal time.

You can see him in his office
Without appointments made ahead,
Or he'll still come to see you
If you're too weak and sick in bed.

His sight or values were never set
By the mighty dollar sign.
To overcharge and get rich quick
Was the last thing on his mind.
He's the most dedicated doctor
This world has ever known.
Oh, what a harvest he will reap
From all the goodness he has sown.

Photo: Courtesy of The Rushville Times

This is a true story that happened to a co-worker and her brother. Needless to say, it is brought up at most family reunions.

Cheryl and the Cycle

Her brother had a cycle.
Its battery was all run down.
He needed help to start it up,
So he could ride to town.

He had Cheryl get into her car,
And then he took a rope.
He tied the cycle to the car,
Yelling, "This will work, I hope!"

It would only take a little pull.
Just enough to get it runnin'.
With glassy eyes, she stared ahead,
Her engine wildly hummin'.

He yelled real loud, "Go about ten."
She quite misunderstood.
"As fast as you can" is what she heard.
She'd do it, if she could.

She squeezed the wheel with sweaty hands.
Pressed the pedal to the floor.
The car gave forth a mighty leap.
She looked back nevermore.

Her brother, at the very start,
Was thrown onto the ground.
The cycle with no rider
Was bouncing all around.

A farmer working in the fields
Saw Cheryl a flying by.
With the motor cycle bouncing
He could only wonder "Why?"

Before they got control of things,
The cycle was a wreck.
And when they had to tell their mom,
She sure did give them heck.

When something doesn't sound quite right,
You should do a second check.
It could have saved that cycle
From one hysterical wreck.

On the way to Illinois this May 22, 2003, I began writing this for my oldest granddaughter, Audra Kay Wilson, who was graduating. I had known for 18 years she was going to graduate, but waited until on the way to her graduation to begin writing a poem for her. I got very little done on the way, but once there, I finished it quickly. I used to video tape her when she was a little girl, and when she came to my house, she would always say, " I want to see Baby Audra, on TV." We still call her "Baby Audra" now and then.

Baby Audra
Photo: Courtesy of Lane Photography

Audra Kay

You came into my life one fall
On a mild November day.
A tiny, perfect baby girl,
And they named you Audra Kay.

A granddaughter, you were my first.
How my heart filled up with love.
A baby sent from heaven,
A gift from God above.

You began to grow, to crawl to walk.
Your school days soon were here.
I tried to hold on tight, but knew
The little girl would disappear.

Time changes things, as the years go by
Like a wild wind in a whirl.
I love the woman you've become,
But I sure miss the little girl.

Your graduation day is drawing near.
I wish all the best for you,
And hope that you find happiness
In everything you do.

May you climb all of your mountains,
May you conquer all your fears.
May your smiles, your joys, your happiness
Outweigh all of your tears.

I love you now and forever,
And as you journey on your way,
Remember you will always be
Your grandma's "Baby Audra Kay."

*Audra (right) is shown on graduation day,
May 27, 2003 with her sister, Kara*

This poem is about being a grandma for the second time. This is dedicated to my second grandson, Justin Glenn David Young.

The Second Child

You can pour your love upon one child
Until your heart is drained and dry.
But you never have to share that love...
God just gives a new supply.

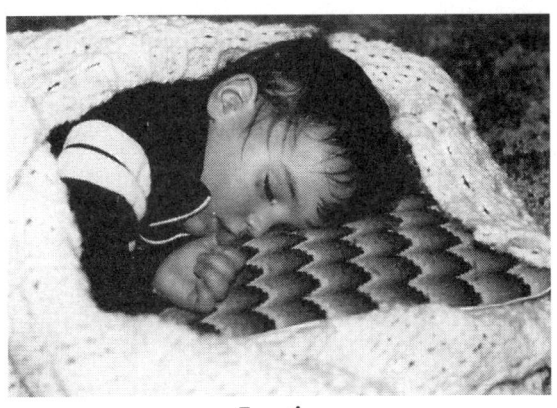

Justin,
Who is now 22 years old

I wrote this poem for my first grandson, Jason Young, on his wedding day, May 19, 2000. He and his wife, Katie, have been married three years and are living in Cedar Rapids, Iowa.

Jason & Katie Young
Photo: Courtesy of Linda Moore

Your Wedding Day

Today you're getting married.
How those years just slipped away.
They changed you from a boy
Into the man you are today.

How I treasure every moment
Of the times I've spent with you.
A thought will sometimes make me smile,
While others make me blue.

Today you're here with loved ones
To take Katie as your wife.
I wish you health and happiness
As you start your brand new life.

May your life be filled forever
With sunshine and skies of blue.
And when they're not, just take God's hand,
He'll always see you through.

Today God has joined you,
For He knows your love is true.
He's entwined your lives together.
Now you're one instead of two.

Eighteen

How can it be you're eighteen,
And you've grown so big and tall?
Did I close my eyes and slumber
Through those years and miss it all?

I don't know when it happened.
I cannot understand.
Time took away the little boy,
Replaced him with a man.

Yesterday you were so tiny,
Dimpled hands and eyes so blue.
I thought my heart would burst with love
The first time I saw you.

I've always been proud of you,
And would like for you to know
That I will always be here for you
Wherever you may go.

You were my first grandchild to love,
And my life you've filled with joy.
You will always be, no matter what,
Your grandma's baby boy.
With love to my first grandson on his 18th birthday.

24

Cheryl Clements visited me one day and asked if I could write a poem about her son, Scott. Scott lost his life in an accident when he was way too young to be called home. I knew who Scott was, but didn't know him personally. I went to Cheryl's one day, and she gave me some details about his life, which I used to write the poem.

Scott Clements

So short his time upon this earth,
'Till Scott was called away.
Though it happened many years ago,
It seems like yesterday.

He felt the premonition.
Told his mother and his friends
He wouldn't live long with them,
That soon his life would end

Scott loved his mom and sisters,
Though young, was still a man.
He had just accepted Jesus
When God took him by the hand.

He heard his mother say one day
She'd like a mother's ring.
He wanted to fulfill that wish of hers
More than any other thing.

He worked and saved his money
Doing jobs with little pay.
He bought that ring for mother,
And she wears it still today.

Scott was good to all who knew him.
It was hard with him to part.
But he will live forever
In a corner of their heart.

CHAPTER
II
LIFE
AND
THOUGHTS

I Know I Can

They hung black clouds above my head,
So dark I could not see.
I shoved them quickly from my sight,
Now, the sun can shine on me.

They put a mountain in my path,
Though I was tired and weak.
I climbed it slowly step by step
Until I reached its highest peak.

They put a river across my road
So very deep and wide.
I took some tools and built a bridge
That reached the other side.

They let it rain on my parade,
But I marched on, head held high,
Until the sun came shining through the clouds
And a rainbow filled my sky.

When obstacles lay in your path
And you're filled with fear and doubt,
Just tell yourself, "I KNOW I CAN!"
That's what life's all about.

They let it rain on my parade......

Life's Highway

While driving down life's highway,
I always went too fast.
Many things were there for me,
But I hurried right on past.
I said, "I'll catch you later,
I'm in a hurry, can't you see?"
But what I didn't realize was
They wouldn't wait for me.

...so don't be going 90 in a 55 speed zone.

Time marches on.
It won't wait for any man.
You've got to take your chances.
You've got to grab them while you can.
You've got to stop, look, and listen,
Or you'll reap the seeds you've sown.
So don't be going 90 in a 55 speed zone.

I saw old opportunity
Down by the overpass.
I didn't want to stop for him,
So I stepped down on the gas.
I just smiled at him and waved
As I passed him by the side.
Oh, if only I had just slowed down
And took him for a ride.

When life finally slows you down
And your road comes to an end,
And you pull off every exit
Just looking for a friend.
You look around and realize
That you are all alone,
'Cause you were going 90
In a 55 speed zone.

Wishing and Wanting

I wished and longed for a trinket.
It was a useless, worthless thing,
But I just knew that it would change my life
From all the happiness it would bring.

I thought about it day and night,
And when I'd go to bed,
Sweet dreams about my trinket
Were spinning in my head.

I'd even go to look at it
In the window at the store.
If only it belonged to me,
I would never ask for more.

The day arrived; it now was mine.
I clutched it to my chest.
Of the many things that filled my life
I loved this one the best.

My yearning days were over,
My dreams had all come true.
But the trinket lay forgotten,
And I was wanting something new.

The challenge now was over,
So I started wishing once again.
When it comes to wants and wishes,
I guess there probably is no end.

I'd even go to look at it in the window at the store...

The One-Armed Bandit

He came riding into our little town
One dark and dreary day.
We'd heard the warning long ago
That he was on his way.

He tied up by the river's edge
Just to play his little game.
He didn't have to wear a mask,
One-armed Bandit was the name.

Folks flocked down there to greet him,
So thrilled to shake his hand.
He's going to make the poor man rich.
There was hardly room to stand.

They came from miles and miles around
Their hopes high as the sky,
But left with empty pockets
In the blinking of an eye.

He's really slick at robbing them.
They never even see the gun.
So caught up with the fever
And having so much fun.

Pawnshops sprang up all over town.
Their lines were long and lean.
The buzzards circled overhead.
Soon bones would be picked clean.

Every now and then a shot rang out,
Or they'd cut a person down.
Yes, everything was on the downhill slide
Since old Bandit came to town.

He has no heart or feelings,
And for what he takes, he gives no thanks.
But you can bet he's smiling big
All the way down to the banks.

An elderly lady had written to an advice columnist about unexpectedly getting pregnant in her forties. When she became pregnant, she asked God why? She felt she hadn't received an answer, but after many years she now knew why. That little girl born to her late in life had taken care of her father and her stepfather until their deaths and was now taking care of the mother. Sometimes God just doesn't answer at the time we would like for Him to, and sometimes the answer we receive is not the one we wanted to hear. The idea for this poem came from that letter.

Middle-Aged Mother

I'm forty-five, and I'm with child.
I cried to God, "oh, why?"
I listened for an answer.
Heard silence, no reply.

I thought those years were over.
My children are all grown.
I need to rest and have some peace,
Some time to be alone.

Very soon a tiny girl was born.
How I loved her from the start.
She wrapped her tiny fingers
Around mine and my heart.

The question soon forgotten,
Oh, how the years did fly.
To think a child, unwanted
Was now the apple of my eye.

Now I am old and very ill.
Like a mother, she gives me care.
And the one I never wanted
When I need her, she is there.

The question I had asked of God
Those many years ago
When I thought He didn't hear me...
It took so long to know.

God knows what lies ahead of us.
We should never question, "Why?"
Sometimes He's slow to answer.
But our needs He does supply.

Both Sides of Life

Some are born with a silver spoon,
Red roses for a bed.
Their pockets lined with silver
And satin pillows for their head.

Their vocabulary is very small.
It's only "I" and "me."
From the tip of their nose
Between their eyes
Is as far as they can see.

Trouble never comes to visit
Or knock upon their door.
They never share or give a dime
To the needy or the poor.

Others are born into poverty,
And that's the way they'll stay.
They can work from morn till setting sun.
Nothing ever goes their way.

They'd give the shirt right off their back.
They're a friend to all mankind.
Not a selfish thought has ever been
In their heart or crossed their mind.

Whenever the door is opened,
Trouble seems to barge right in.
No matter what they say or do,
They can't get rid of him.

Is our life a plan we cannot change?
To try would mean defeat.
Will we never waltz to a different tune
Or march to a different beat?

Some people seem to have it all.
Others only know despair.
But like we've heard a million times,
"Life isn't always fair."

My Rainbow's Treasure

I stood alone, filled with despair,
From out of nowhere, he was there.
He held me close and took my hand.
Said, "Please don't cry, I understand.
I know the hurt. I feel your pain.
I've seen the storms, I've felt the rain."

As he held me, oh, so tight,
The dark clouds left, the sun shone bright.
A rainbow filled my life and sky,
The storm was calm. My eyes were dry.
The treasure found at my rainbow's end,
Worth more than gold, it was a friend.

My Handprints

I'm leaving you my handprints
Because I'm growing fast.
And soon my tiny fingers
Will be memories of the past.

Now when I'm big and leave you,
And if we're far apart,
You can look and see my fingers,
And feel them touch your heart.

Life's Pages

If our lives were but a story
In a book, page after page,
And we had the power to turn them back
To any time or age.
All the mistakes that we had made
In our life we could erase,
And all the pain and sorrow
We'd never had to face.
But you never get that second chance,
So think before you act.
Once those pages have been turned,
There's no way going back.

If our lives knew only happy days
And our skies were always blue,
And we never had to face black clouds
When the storms of life rolled through.
If we never felt a burning tear
Or rain upon our face,
And our life was full of sunshine,
And our world a perfect place....
Then we'd never know or understand
As we journeyed life's pathways
That to grow in courage, faith, and love,
We need those stormy days.

The Seed

The seed lay dormant in the ground,
Sleeping there so very sound.
Dropped last fall from her mother's womb.
Covered by earth like a cold dark tomb.
Sleeping through long winter days.
Waiting for the sun's warm rays.
At last the days of spring arrived,
She awoke, stretched, then rubbed her eyes.
When reaching up to touch the sun
This thing called life, had now begun.
She pushed her head up through the ground.
Stood very small, looked all around.
Began to grow so big and tall.
Summer passed, then came the fall.
She'd borne her fruit and now she knew
Her days to live were very few.
Her leaves were dying, turning brown,
And her seed lay scattered on the ground.
The wheels of nature begin to spin,
And the cycles repeated once again.
Man and seed you can compare,
But there's more to man then we see here.
We live and die, though our body's gone,
Unlike the seed, our soul lives on.

Upon Graduation

You stand in front of a brand-new bridge,
Leaving the old one far behind.
You will never travel it again,
You can do it just one time.

Many roads and bridges lie ahead,
And decisions you must make.
It all depends on the journey's end
By the ones you chose to take.

As you travel down the road of life,
You may stumble, even fall.
Though many battles you will fight,
You'll never win them all.

You may be down and beaten,
Don't just lay there and bleed.
Stand up tall. Take one more step.
You must do so to succeed.

Some will travel, oh, so far,
While others stop to rest.
But your life will be successful
If you always do your best.

Don't try to base your success
By your money, house, or car,
But how you treat your fellow man
And how happy that you are.

Try to make your memories happy ones.
Be loving, and be kind.
Be a friend to everyone you meet,
And leave your enemies behind.

Just work and sweat, give and love,
So when you're laid to rest,
That they can write upon your stone:
"He always did his best."

You stand in front of a brand new bridge........

This poem sounds like it could have been written about one of the school shootings, but it was written many years before any of them.

The Unloved Child

The child was born on a cold dark night.
The moon and the stars hid their face from the sight
Of an unloved child.

He was born to a family, oh so fine,
Who had the money but not the time
To give this child.

He was never held nor rocked, but fed
By a bottle propped in a lonely bed.
This lonely child.

He grew up lanky, cold and mean.
But he's just a normal, typical teen
The mother smiled.

But that smile has since been erased
By tears of sorrow running down her face
And across her heart.

He went off on a killing spree.
He turned the gun, fell to his knee.
Left this world.

The reason why was never known.
Was the fault really his alone?
This unloved child.

A child's a gift from God above.
If nothing else, give him love.
This precious child.

Memories of a House

The house sits almost hidden,
In a lonely forgotten place.
He thinks and dreams of the family
Once held in his embrace.

His windows cracked and broken,
Doors lying on the ground.
The shutters blown by many a storm
Lie scattered all around.

48

In days gone by, a young man once
Carried through those doors his bride.
All new and happy was the house,
Watching the young man beam with pride.

One cold and stormy winter night,
With the north wind blowing wild.
The house smiled, knowing he would soon
Hear the laughter of a child.

More babies later came along;
The family now was five.
Love and happiness filled the house,
Making him vibrant and alive.

The favorite part of the day he thought,
Was before they went to bed.
They gathered around, said their prayers,
And from the Bible they all read.

It happened in the wintertime,
Though the day was very mild.
The man came running toward the house,
Carrying the limp form of his child.

The child was skating on the pond...
What a lovely day to skate.
He heard the cracking of the ice,
By then it was too late.

They chose a place behind the house
So the child would be close by.
Was it rain running down his window panes,
Or can a house actually cry?

Nothing ever seemed the same again.
Laughter was seldom heard.
The family moved about the rooms,
Very seldom spoke a word.

All too soon the children, grown
Moved to places far away.
The bride and groom, left all alone
Are old and bent and gray.

Behind the house, next to their child,
The couple lie beneath their stone.
The house unloved and empty,
Dies slowly all alone.

The unkempt yard grows wild with weeds
Where children used to run.
Trees grow so tall, around the house
He can hardly see the sun.

How he longed to feel and hear the sound
Of feet across his floor.
Now silence echoes through the house.
Those sounds he'll hear no more.

One by one, the children return
To be laid there with the rest.
The sun keeps rising in the east
And goes down in the west.

The houses has so many memories.
How he longs for those happy days.
When his walls echoed children's laughter
Now forever gone away.

Summer Fun in the 1940's

When we were kids, we used to lay
On a blanket on the ground.
We'd watch the white and fluffy clouds
Pass by without a sound.

In days gone by, this simple thing
Could be a child's delight:
Just to look above at floating clouds,
Trying to guess what they looked like.

With no TVs or fancy games,
We created our own fun.
Before Mom let us run and play,
Our chores must all be done.

Sometimes we walked out to the woods,
To gather nuts there in the fall.
Catch minnows in a nearby creek
Or play a game of ball.

When it got dark, it was in our yard
The neighbor kids would come.
We'd play a game of Kick the Can.
It was always so much fun.

When we got tired of playing games,
We'd find an old fruit jar
And fill it full of lightning bugs
Or make wishes on a star.

We'd jump hop scotch, play Simon Says,
Play marble games for hours.
The first day in the month of May,
We'd make baskets full of flowers.

If only I had a time machine
That could take me back to then.
I'd love to have those fun-filled days
To live over once again.

So busy were those days of youth
In those summer days so hot.
Then you ask the question, "Were you bored?"
Most certainly we were not!

What does that cloud look like?

The Time that Got Away

I arose from bed this morning.
Had hardly turned around.
My work lay there unfinished,
And the sun was going down.

Is time really going faster,
Or am I just slowing down?
I often ask this question,
But no answer have I found.

It seems I'm not the only one
That at the end of every day,
Just shakes their head and wonders
About their time that got away.

I believe we have all used the excuse, "I sure have thought about you," when we run into someone that we have failed to do anything for, when they needed action instead of just thoughts.

Thoughts or Actions

To give someone a pleasant thought
Is indeed very kind.
But what we need is action
Because we cannot read your mind.

Thinking of You

Every now and then
I think of you
But how are you to know.
Because I never write
Or send a card,
Or call to tell you so.

But today I stopped
And took the time,
And all I want to say,
Is if only for a little while,
I thought of you today.

Forgiving

"Let bygones be bygones."
We've all heard this before.
Just put your hurts in one big room,
Then leave and lock the door.

Take the key and get rid of it.
Just throw it far away.
Your heart will feel much lighter.
Do it NOW, without delay.

Someday you may pass by that room
And pause before that door.
But once you've closed and locked it tight,
You must enter it no more.

Perhaps the one who caused you pain
Is even unaware.
And the fact that you've forgiven them,
Well, they don't really care.

You must forgive them for yourself.
You must do it to survive.
Having hurt and anger in your life
Can eat you up alive.

So let bygones be bygones.
You are the one set free.
Your life will be much happier.
Just do it, and you'll see.

Ten Feet Tall

When you were young, you thought you were
Bulletproof and ten feet tall.
Not a soul could tell you anything.
You thought you knew it all.

You told your parents many times:
"My life, it is my own.
I can do anything I want with it.
Just please leave me alone!"

You did "your thing" for several years.
Took the bull right by the horn.
When your parents tried to give advice,
You stared at them with scorn.

So they stepped back, never leaving you,
Just giving you your space.
But if you ever needed them,
They'd be there, just in case.

You got into some problems deep.
Had to swallow all your pride.
Your parents said you could move home,
But their rules you must abide.

No one ever lives a perfect life.
Everyone will make mistakes,
And some, we've said, when doing well
Just had some lucky breaks.

Life is not a dress rehearsal.
It is the actual play.
Perhaps from others we could learn,
Though it may not be our way.

When you have children of your own,
Then you will know it's true.
How much easier you could make their life,
If they would only learn from you.

School of Hard Knocks

I've graduated once again
From the college of hard knocks.
You can go there anytime you like.
It has no doors or locks.

I'm going to take my diploma
And hang it with the rest.
I have a whole wall full of them.
I've passed every single test.

I know many who have been there.
Some names I can recall.
I've sat with you in class before
Or passed you in the hall.

I'm so full of knowledge and advice,
I don't know what to do.
The question, I must ask myself
Is, "Who do I give it to?"

I could have saved some from their fate,
But to me no one would listen.
They had to do it their own way
For fear something was missin'.

Everyone must make their own mistakes,
While their whole world shakes and rocks.
And soon they, too, will graduate
From the college of hard knocks.

The Barn Then and Now

The farmer built a mighty barn.
He painted it bright red.
Filled it full of straw and hay
So his animals could be fed.

The cows were brought there to be milked.
The horses came to sleep.
Animals filled its many rooms.
There were chickens, hogs, and sheep.

Both the farmer and the barn grew old.
Its red had turned to gray.
The house burned down just last year,
So the farmer moved away.

After that, the years flew quickly by.
How many? He'd lost track.
He missed the farmer and his friends.
He longed to have them back.

In youth, he was the mightiest barn
For miles and miles around.
Now rendered useless and decayed,
Soon they would tear him down.

A summer storm began to brew.
Lightning flashed across the sky.
Two lovers, walking through the woods,
Happened to be passing by.

They spied the barn and ran inside
As the rain began to pour.
The barn again felt warmth inside
Like he had felt before.

The storm soon passed. The sky turned blue.
The lovers walked away.
The barn felt happiness once again
On that rainy summer day.

Make Children Mind

He always was a bratty child,
Was never made to mind.
It was easier to give in to him
When he threw his fits or whined.

When very small this was "so cute,"
But what they didn't realize
Was that a monster was being formed
Right before their eyes.

Whenever children played with him,
He bullied them around.
And always managed one more kick
After he had knocked them down.

During all his years of growing up,
His folks were seldom home.
They were busy with their social life,
So he spent his time alone.

They worked two jobs to give him things
That they had never had.
A big mistake most parents make,
But it seems the going fad.

64

They seemed so shocked, could not believe,
When the cops or school would call.
About this child they hardly knew
And very seldom saw.

It seemed the only way that he
Could make them notice him
Was to rage a daily battle
To see just who would win.

People want to give their children much,
But the best thing they could do
Is give them time and make them mind.
I wish I had, don't you?

Returning Love

There are many things in this old world
That simply can't be done.
To make somebody love you,
Well, that's probably number one.

You can swim the deepest ocean
Or climb the mountains high,
But you cannot make them love you,
No matter how you try.

If you tried to make a list of things
Done in the "name of love."
It would reach from here around the world
And to the moon above.

You can love someone with all your heart,
But it's a well-known fact
That just because you love them
Doesn't mean they love you back.

If just once in your whole lifetime
Somebody loves you true,
Then you should thank the Lord above
For giving them to you.

This thing called love, it works both ways,
It's not a one-way street.
And there are times when the shoes you wear
Are on the other feet.

You, too, can give your love away
And get none in return.
It's a part of life, or so they say,
"Some people never learn."

If two can find a mutual love,
Just grab it up and run,
And when you do, then you will know
Your life has just begun.

About the Summum Curve

Living beside the Summum curve was about as exciting as it got when you grew up in an Illinois town of 200 people during the 1940's. The poem and stories that follow are just some things that I remember about the town.

One of my most vivid memories is a fatal accident that happened on the sharp curve. The night it happened, my siblings and I were awakened by Mom, who was usually hysterical about most things, serious or not. It was around 2 a.m. when Dad heard the semi braking. He knew it wouldn't make the curve. Dad claimed he was up and dressed before it ever hit. He tried to get the driver out but was unsuccessful.

There was a possibility that our house would catch fire, so we all left the house and spent the night in the yard, watching the fire burn. A neighbor's garage did catch fire. The semi, which had been carrying cookies and crackers, burned for the rest of the night. As a young girl, I tried to be where any action was, so I was there when they cut the driver out.

A tragedy like that leaves a lasting memory. Later, the driver's father came to see where the accident had happened. I remember him saying, "I just hope that he was dead when it hit." He was assured that he was. The main highway no longer passes through Summum.

The Summum Curve

I was born and raised in Summum,
A town so very small.
If you never left Route 24,
You nearly missed it all.

On Route 24 was a big sharp curve
At the edge of our small town.
A great big crash or thud was heard
Every time you turned around.

Late one night way after dark...
Nineteen-fifty was the year.
A semi didn't make the curve
And filled the night with fear.

Dad said he heard brakes squealing.
He would never forget the sound
Of metal crashing against a tree,
Waking up most of the town.

He ran down as quickly as he could
To see what he could do.
The doors could not be opened.
Hot flames began to spew.

Immediately, it was a ball of fire.
The flames were shooting high.
All you could do was stand and stare,
Thinking they may reach the sky.

Fire trucks were called from miles around.
All through the night it burned.
Some were afraid they'd lose their homes.
The whole town was concerned.

By the time the sun was coming up,
Everyone had all gone home.
Even the driver of that big old truck,
Who sat there all alone.

Though I was just a little girl,
I'll never forget the sight.
God called home the driver of that truck
On the Summum curve that night.

Stories About the Summum Curve

Another bad accident happened when a vehicle ran into an elderly couple's home. They were knocked out of bed and injured. I am not sure how badly they were injured, but I do remember one or both of them had broken ribs. The home had been converted from an old filling station that sat about halfway around the curve, really close to the highway. Some time later, another man moved into the old filling station and converted the front part into a tavern and lived in the back.

~~~~~~

My youngest sister, Connie, who was about five at the time, was where she shouldn't have been. A car saw her coming and stopped, but Connie didn't. She was running head down, I guess, so SHE hit the car. Again, Mom was hysterical.

71

One summer day, Mom was hanging out clothes on the clothesline while the twins were playing on a blanket nearby. Suddenly, a huge tire came rolling through the yard, barely missing her and the babies. It had come off a truck going around the curve. Yep, Mom was hysterical.

~~~~~~

In 1975, my sister Thelma worked for the John Onion filling station store. As she was washing windows, the band on a truckload of plywood snapped. The plywood crashed through the windows of the store. Had she been at the register, where she usually was, she would have been either injured or killed.

~~~~~~

Onion's store was also Summum's bus stop. Whenever the driver was almost to town, he would shout: "SUMMUM. SOME ON ONE SIDE AND SOME ON THE OTHER."

Summum is the name I use for my email account and in Web chat rooms. Many people in the chat rooms thought I was from England and that the word Summum meant good mother ("some Mum"). I hope someday to write about my memories of the people and town of Summum. Days like those are gone forever, and all we have are the memories to pass on to our future generations.

~~~~~~

I also have many happy memories from the Summum curve. In the summer we had free picture shows. There were two large poles placed on a lot. On the night of the movie, a large canvas screen was stretched between the poles. People sat in cars, chairs, or on blankets on the ground. Movies always drew large crowds.

One time, the church was taking the youth group to the St. Louis Zoo. My younger brother, Dale, who was about 10 then, refused to go because a Hopalong Cassidy movie was playing that evening and he wasn't about to miss it. The rest of us went to the zoo and were back in time to see the movie.

The Summum Curve

Even a movie star was born on the Summum curve: Smiley Burnett. His former home is still there. I know the younger generation reading this is saying, "Who the heck is Smiley Burnett?" He was Gene Autry's side-kick. If you don't know who Gene Autry is, ask your parents. Smiley later played the conductor on Petticoat Junction.

When I was young, Smiley came to town. It doesn't take long for word to spread in a small town, and soon he was surrounded by Summumites. He was shown through his old house, and I was told that he wrote this on the bedroom wall: "Smiley Burnett was born in this room." Rumor has it that the people living there papered around it for years.

Birthplace of Smiley Burnett
Summum, Illinois

Put Into a Bottle

Have you ever felt like you were put
Into a bottle and sealed tight?
Then tossed into the sea of life
And drifting out of sight.

The only thing that you can see
Is water all around.
Every now and then a ship will pass,
But you are never found.

The sun would shine on you all day,
But you knew the night would come.
The moon gave out a bit of light,
Yet you longed to see the sun.

When the darkness came, it seemed as if
It would never go away.
You fear you'll never feel again
Or see the light of day.

Most days at sea were very calm,
But you knew without a doubt
That storms would come and in the sea
You'd be thrown and tossed about.

Perhaps you've set your goals too low,
Or maybe way too high.
So you stare out through your bottle,
Watching life just pass you by.

Sooner or later it will happen.
You finally see the light.
And know that when you reach the shore
Everything will be all right.

Your destiny always takes you
Where you are meant to be.
And when it does you'll know at last
That from the bottle you are free.

Years ago, while attending a Dairy Queen® convention, I heard the phrase, "I can honestly say I have had a love affair with Dairy Queen," from one of the speakers. He went on to say he had owned and operated a Dairy Queen for over 20 years and he had loved every minute of getting up and going to work. A couple of years later that line surfaced in my mind, and I wrote this poem.

I also want to dedicate this to all of my employees who worked for me the 33 years that I managed the Rushville Dairy Queen. I had so many faithful, hard working employees and I never could have done it without them.

My Love Affair With Dairy Queen®

Since I was just a little kid,
I've loved that DQ® cone.
My mom would give me just a dime,
And I'd go there all alone.
I'd buy myself the biggest cone
That you have ever seen,
'Cause I've always had a love affair
With my hometown Dairy Queen®

I grew up fast and went to school,
But stopped most every day,
For I had fallen deep in love
I could not stay away.
It was there I started working
When I was just sixteen.
Yes, I've always had a love affair
With my hometown Dairy Queen.

I graduated and moved away,
But like I always knew
That I would own a Dairy Queen,
Or maybe even two.
A Dairy Queen of my very own
Was an answer to a dream,
'Cause I've always had a love affair
With my hometown Dairy Queen.

I've been here, oh, so many years,
My grandchildren are grown.
So many people I have met
And so many I have known.
I'm still in love with DQ;
Nothing could ever come between,
Yes, I've always had a love affair
With my hometown Dairy Queen.

When I die and go to heaven,
in the sweet by and by,
And go to that big Dairy Queen
Way up there in the sky.
A Dairy Queen on every cloud
Will landscape heaven's scene,
And I'll be in love forever
With my heavenly Dairy Queen.

Three Little Words

Why are the words, "I love you"
For some, so hard to say?
When you share your life with someone,
You need to tell them every day.
They may be feeling sad and blue
Or just a wee bit down.
Those three little words will make them smile
And wipe away their frown.
"I love you," will touch their heart,
Warm their soul, through and through.
Just walk up, and make their day
By saying, "I love you!"

Judging

Some people cannot see beyond
Another's flesh and bone.
Just how narrow is their mind?
Is their heart made out of stone?

To judge a person at first sight
And never realize
Most beauty lies much deeper
Than a person's looks or size.

So sad the things they could have had
But they were much too blind
So see a kind and caring heart,
Perhaps a brilliant mind.

In times of need, you never know
On who you can depend.
Of all the things you may have lost,
It probably was a friend.

CHAPTER III

WAR AND RELIGION

Picture composed by: M. L. S.

Then he opened up his black book and read the names
he written down............

The Battle

The battle cry was sounded.
Sweaty hands gripped tight his gun.
The young man knew that he must charge,
Though fear made him want to run.

He heard bullets flying overhead
When he saw the great black horse.
Death sat high in the saddle.
His voice loud and coarse.

"I'll not be cheated," he screamed out,
As his horse pawed at the ground.
Then he opened up his big black book
And read the names he'd written down.

As the horse approached, the young man stared
Into the face of Death,
Who now so close that he could feel
The hot sting of his breath.

Black and hollow eyes stared back.
His hand was reaching out.
Soon Death would have him in his grip.
Not for a moment did he doubt.

The soldier dropped before Death.
Was now on bended knees.
His fear replaced by faith in God,
Cried out to God, "Oh please!"

"Please save me, almighty God.
Don't let me die this day.
I have a wife, a little girl,
And another on the way."

Then God, in all his mercy,
Opened the gate to heaven wide.
Sent down a band of angels
To be by the young man's side.

The angels circled around him
On that blood-soaked battle ground.
They lifted up and carried him
Far from the battle sound.

Death rode by where the young man stood,
And softly he heard him say,
"You were saved by the grace of God!"
Then he turned and rode away.

The Problem with Wars

He lies on the ground
In the cold and the mud.
His shirt was all soaked
With his sweat and his blood.
Just short days ago
Mother bid him goodbye.
She held him and kissed him
Tried hard not to cry.
He had not a quarrel
With friend or with foe.
When he heard there was war,
He knew he must go.
As the cold winds of war
Swept across the dark land,
Though still just a boy,
He died like a man.
The problem with wars,
And we'll never know why,
Is it's old men who cause them,
But young men who die.

God the Author

Suppose that God would advertise
That He was going to be
On earth to autograph His Book,
The B-I-B-L-E.

He'd be at your local Bible store
Each day to sign His name.
Oh, what if no one even showed,
Wouldn't it be a shame?

You've seen the lines at ball games,
At concerts, and the show.
Do you think they'll stand in line for God,
Someone they hardly know?

Most folks would probably wonder:
"Where did I put that Book?"
In every drawer and shelf around
They'd probably have to look.

And when the Book is finally found,
The dust would surely fly,
Or else they'd have to run to town,
So a Bible they could buy.

But wouldn't it be so wonderful,
When upon God's face you look
That you could stare Him in the eye
And say, "Hey, I've read your book!"

The angel took him back to God......

Jesus Cried

A tiny unborn baby died.
Oh how Jesus must have cried.
His heart so full of grief and pain
That tears fell down like drops of rain.
The child could only question, "Why?"
To be conceived, then have to die.
The angels took him back to God.
His feet on earth would never trod.
If only they had let him live
And to another woman give.
Who prays each day to God above
For just a child to have and love.
A precious gift of God was lost.
Was it really worth the cost?

A Soldier Writes Home

Dear Mom, I'm in a trench tonight.
It's rained; the mud is deep.
I'm wet and cold, chilled to the bone,
So tired, but cannot sleep.

The battle has been raging long,
Screams and bullets pierce the air.
I want to be home safe with you.
Dear God, it's so unfair.

To go to war in this foreign land.
To fight, perhaps to die.
I'm choked from holding back the tears,
'Cause big boys just don't cry.

I bow my head and close my eyes,
Pretending I am home.
I know your prayers are with me, Mom.
God's here, I'm not alone.

You raised me in a Christian home,
And I've walked with God each day.
If an angel should be sent for me,
I must go. I cannot stay.

If from this war I don't return,
And when your work is done,
We'll meet again on heaven's shore.
I love you Mom, Your son.

Blue and Gray

They drew a line right straight through
That cut our country half in two.
One wore gray; one wore blue.

They wore their colors with much pride.
Brothers fighting on each side.
For their cause they fought and died.

When everything was said and done,
Had either side really won?
So many mothers lost a son.

When a nation divides all must pay
And the wounds are healing still today.
One wore blue; one wore gray.

CHAPTER IV
THE "LITE" SIDE DIETING

Procrastinating

Tomorrow I'll start my diet.
I can't possibly start today.
I just baked a big old chocolate cake,
And there's a pizza on the way.

It may even start MUCH later.
I always seem to hesitate.
There's so much food around the house,
My diet will have to wait.

There are chips hidden in the cupboard.
Cookies in the cookie jar.
I thought I'd found a treasure
When I spied that candy bar.

If you'd like a piece of apple pie,
Let me give you some advice:
You don't have to count the calories
If it's just a real small slice.

They told me I should walk a lot.
Heck, I did that anyway.
I walk over to my fridge at least
A hundred times a day.

I really need to lose those pounds.
I hope I find a way.
More diets seem to start tomorrow
Then they ever do today.

Counting and Counting

I've tried counting carbohydrates.
I've counted calories, too.
I've counted sodium, fiber, fat....
What more can I do?

The ounces of water that I drink,
I've even counted that.
I weigh and measure, count, count, count
But still I am too fat.

Even when I go to bed at night,
I lie there counting sheep.
I wouldn't be a bit surprised
If I counted in my sleep.

I count and count but never lose.
By night I then now know why.
For the numbers when I add them up,
The totals are too high.

Food We Love

When our thoughts turn to food,
Oh, why, must it be?
The one we love most,
Is our worst enemy!

We've all heard the expression, "It's not what you eat, but what is eating you." The next poem was written with that in mind.

Eating Problems

I had problems,
They ate away at me.
The more they ate away,
The larger I became.
Very soon,
Being larger
Was a problem
That was eating
Away at me.

The Health Nut

She got up every morning
Before the sun arose.
Put on her little tennis shoes
And her favorite jogging clothes.

She'd stretch a bit, then out the door
To jog a mile or two.
To live a long and healthy life,
This is a must to do.

After punching out at five o'clock,
She drove directly to the gym.
Did aerobics for the next two hours
To keep her firm and trim.

When shopping at the grocery store
It would take a lot of time.
To read and study labels
And watch for low fat signs.

She never bought or ate junk food,
Or so it has been said.
She wouldn't put it in her mouth
With a gun held to her head.

She bought her many vitamins
By the case and by the ton.
You could go right down the list of them,
She had every single one.

She did all this and much, much more
To stay healthy, trim, and lean,
But these things make little difference
When you drive a mean machine.

She jumped into her car one day
Her fiber plus was low.
Put the pedal to the metal.
Man, that car could really go.

A healthy driver but too fast.
This is where the story ends.
Although it's big and made of steel,
Around a tree, a Mercedes Benz.

Losing and Winning

They say it doesn't matter
If you win or if you lose,
But you can have it both ways,
If that is what you choose.
You can lose those ugly pounds,
And you will be much thinner.
The person in the mirror will say,
"So you lost, but you're a winner!"

CHAPTER V
HUMOR

*As the next poem says, I entered a poetry contest adver-
tised in the newspaper. Supposedly, there was prize money
involved. The answer I received from the publishing com-
pany is the subject of this poem. I learned to be careful
about entering contests. The company wanted to publish
my work and then sell it back to me in a book. No thanks.
I wrote this poem and mailed it back to them. I am sure
they filed it under, "Things to Read and Laugh at on a
Boring Day."*

Not Paying to Publish

I read it in the paper:
A contest there will be
Where I could win some money
For writing poetry.

So I sat right down and wrote a poem
And mailed it off that day.
Waited patiently for an answer
To see what they would say.

They said that they would publish
My poem...and right away.....
But before this can happen
I had to pay, and pay, and pay.

If there's anything about myself
In this book, I'd like to say,
Well, they ain't a gonna print it
Unless I pay, and pay and pay.

If I'd like to dedicate my poem,
There's only one sure way;
Just dig down in my pocket
And pay, and pay, and pay.

They'll even make me a copy
Just to keep, or give away,
But you've already guessed it,
I'd have too pay, and pay, and pay.

You can bet that they will publish
Any poem or words I say
If I just have the money
To pay, and pay, and pay.

I'm sure that they have fooled
A lot of people in their day,
But this here won't be one of them
'Cause I ain't a gonna pay.

Talk is Cheap

Talk is cheap.
You can buy it anywhere.
You can get it at the five and dime,
Even at the county fair.
You can get it at old Wally World
At a discount price.
It's not only been reduced,
But it's been marked down twice.

Just What is Normal?

There's nothing wrong with being
Average or just plain,
Or to be a wee bit flaky,
Or a notch or two from sane.
There's nothing wrong with folks
Who can blend into a crowd
But get their message to the world
Without being rowdy, mean, or loud.
But when you dress or act so differently
For attention or for show,
If you can't at least be normal,
Try to be above...not below.

When THEY say that something's normal,
What exactly do THEY mean?
And when THEY say, "You've crossed the line."
What line do THEY mean?
And while we're asking questions,
"Who the heck are THEY?"
I don't think I've ever met them,
But THEY sure have a lot to say.

Midwest Winters

I jumped up this morning,
All ready to go.
Heard the weatherman say,
"Hey, it's twenty below."
I looked out the window
And shivered a mite.
It sure must have snowed
All through the night.
My car has to be
That big mound of snow,
Or else the home
Of some lost Eskimo.

When I went to bed,
It was really quite warm.
I had not a clue
There would be such a storm.
I shut off the phone
As I jumped back in bed.
Pulled the covers right up
And over my head.
I hope that no one
Through deep snow would travel
To knock on my door,
'Cause nerves to unravel.
I'll just stay in bed.
Pretend not to hear.
Hope they get cold
And soon disappear.
I may stay inside
And not do a thing
Until I hear a robin
And know that it's spring.

Fixing Broken Hearts

If your heart gets cracked or broken,
I can tell you what to do.
There's just one thing to fix it with
That'll make it good as new.

Go buy a roll of duct tape.
It works better than any glue.
Duct tape can fix most anything,
And it'll fix your heart up, too.

It comes in pretty colors now,
So it will look real nice.
Just wrap your heart in duct tape.
I think this will suffice.

Just wrap your heart in duct tape......

The Last Child Raised

The last child's raised and out the door.
You're so happy you're deranged.
You run out and buy new locks
And quickly get them changed.

If they return, their keys won't fit,
So they cannot get in.
But that happy feeling is short lived,
For you turn, and there sits "HIM!"

The man you married long ago
You thought his mother raised
Was just a job passed on to you
To continue…. all your days.

So don't get too excited, Moms
When your last child's out the door.
'Cause as long as you have a husband,
You have a child forever more.

Setting Your Mind to It

I just know that I can do it,
Because it has been said
All I have to do is set my mind
And it's all full steam ahead.

I've been working on this problem now
For about a week or so.
But I have made my mind up
I'd like for you to know.

I think it's really going slow.
It may take quite awhile.
So, I'll just bite my bottom lip
And somehow try to smile.

I know how Mr. Edison felt.
He worked on things for years.
But me, I know in one more day
I'll be reduced to tears.

"You can do anything you want to do."
Well, I have had enough.
This thing I thought that I could do,
For me is just too tough.

The person who said that silly thing,
His brain could use some lube.
I'll bet he never tried to put
Toothpaste back into the tube.

I'll bet he never tried to put toothpaste back into the tube

One early April day in Rushville, Illinois, snow was falling, covering all of the lovely blooming flowers. I was talking to my neighbor, Eileen Estes on the phone, and she suggested I write a poem about the spring snow. Afterwards, I sat down, wrote this poem, and called our local newspaper. The editor took some pictures and published the poem beside them in the paper that week.

April Snow

Wintertime was finally over.
Everywhere we looked was spring.
The daffodils were blooming.
You could hear the robins sing.

Lawn mowers hummed in rhythm.
Kites were flying everywhere.
Young couples strolled together.
Yes, spring was in the air.

Coats and hats were put away.
Thermostats were all turned down.
So shocked were we to look and see
Snow falling to the ground.

It's not nice to fool Mother Nature.
She could cause a real big fuss.
Though she must think it's funny
When she plays her tricks on us.

I Quit

My cookin' days are over.
I ain't a gonna cook no more.
What used to be so fun to do
Is now a tiresome chore.

It seems that man is hungry
Every time he comes through the door.
Well, he might as well get used to it,
'Cause I ain't a gonna cook no more.

I'll box up all my pots and pans
And all my dishes, too.
Have the Salvation Army pick them up,
'Cause my cookin days are through.

The stove and fridge just take up space.
I will try to get them sold.
All I need is a small ice chest
To keep my drinks ice cold.

Either I am going to hire a cook
Or else we'll just eat out,
'Cause I ain't a gonna cook no more.
These words I want to shout!

I want to tell the whole wide world:
"My cookin days are done!
At last, you see, I am set free!
Now I'm gonna have some fun!"

The Auction

I went to an auction just for fun
And to pass some time away.
I wasn't going to buy or bid
For I had no plans to stay.

The auctioneer was winding up.
Excitement grew within the crowd.
They began to bid and wave their arms
And yell their bids out loud.

Then a "thing" was held into the air
That sort of caught my eye.
The crowd was in a frenzy now
As the bids were getting high.

I didn't know just what it was,
But it must be quite a buy,
For if everyone was wanting it,
Then surely so must I.

I was trying hard to keep control.
To bid, I didn't dare.
I don't remember doing it,
But my arm was in the air.

I was caught up in the bidding now
As if my mind, I'd lost.
I was going to have this thing, or else.
No matter what the cost.

Only two of us were bidding now.
My breath, I tried to hold.
Then the auctioneer pointed right at me,
Yelling, "GOING, GOING, SOLD!"

I went to the bank on my way home
For some savings to take out.
A treasure I had found at last
I knew without a doubt.

I knew I had to take it to
That antique appraisal show.
To see just what its value was
I couldn't wait to know.

I stood in line about a half a day.
At last, it was my time.
I'll never forget those words he said,
"This isn't worth a dime."

It took my breath. I needed air.
For the exit made a dash.
But before I left I did one more thing.
I tossed my treasure in the trash.

I tossed my treasure in the trash.

One year before Christmas the UPS truck delivered a package from my sister. She had written on it, "Do not open until Christmas." When I wrote her a thank you note for the gift, I did it in the form of this poem.

An Early Christmas Gift

Santa came to my house.
I knew he surely would
"Cause I've done nuttin' all year long
But try to be real good."

I never cussed or screamed or yelled.
I'm really good I am.
So Santa sent this package,
Not by sleigh but by the UPSEE man.

Santa said he'd been too busy.
It was the best that he could do.
It sure beats having reindeer poop
On your roof and down your flue.

I've already got my present,
So ask me if I care.
"Cause I don't have to be real good
For another day this year."

This was written all in fun. We were discussing funerals at work one day. (Don't ask me, "Why?") I spoke up and said that I would just save my money and hire mourners. Another girl said, "If you want to have a big funeral, have it here at the restaurant." Sooooo..... here is the poem about that conversation.

Hiring Mourners

I have no friends,
So that is why
I'll have to hire mourners
When I die.
It would be so sad
When the deed was done
To be at a funeral
In a crowd of one.
If that's not enough,
We'll hand out treats
And hire cops to handle
The crowds in the streets.
There'll be burgers and fries,
And all you can eat,
At the fun filled funeral
On West Clinton Street.

There'll be no music
To fill the air,
'Cause the radio's been broken
Since way last year.
There'll be no flowers,
For many a reason.
Unless I go
In dandelion season.
There'll be no food brought in,
Only the opposite, and so
Most people will say,
"I'll take mine to go!"
If you like this idea
And have plenty of dough,
To a funeral like this
I'd sure like to go.

Yard Sale Blues

Before I lay me down to sleep,
I must decide which things to keep.
I try to part with them each time.
Even list them on the yard sale sign.

What if I need these things tomorrow?
I'd have to buy or even borrow.
As time draws near, I fill with doubt.
Can I let go? Can I do without?

One by one, I take them back.
Here's Tommy's train, but not the track.
Oh, here is Little Suzie's doll.
She loved it so when she was small.

The dress is dirty, old and torn.
She got that doll when she was born.
There's just one eye on Sally's cat.
She used to sleep each night with that.

These little books, I read each night.
Tucked them in, turned out the light.
Too many things that I hold dear.
My eyes fill up; I wipe a tear.

I may try again at a later date,
But the sale for now, will have to wait.

Before Valentine's Day several years ago, a man had published a nice Valentine poem to his wife in the paper. He wrote about how wonderful she was and all that she did for him. My co-workers and I started talking about what if the same man had a really bad wife and had written a poem about her. This is a satirical poem about the bad wife. It was written all in and for fun, so I hope it makes at least some of you smile.

~~~~~~~~~~~~~~~~~~~~~~~~~~~~~~~~~~~~~~

To My Wife with Love, on Valentine's Day

Speaking of wives,
Let me have my say
To all of you lovers
On Valentine's Day.
Mine's a sight to behold,
And there's really no doubt
She's had me in debt
Since we started out.
She watches TV
And sleeps half the day,
While the kids wreck the house
During their play.

With the dirty dishes
And the dirty clothes,
You can't walk in
Without holding your nose.
When it comes to cooking,
Well, lots of luck.
You'd find better food
On a garbage truck.
Her hair's a mess
And she don't fix her face.
To be seen with her anywhere
Would be a disgrace.
To give her a rating
Would make me a hero,
But they don't make numbers
Lower than zero.
She whines and complains
From morning till night.
When I walk in the house,
There's always a fight.
There are men who have
Lovely wives, yes indeed.
But they picked a flower,
And I picked a weed.

She's put on the wrinkles
And put on the pounds,
So I leave for work early
Without making a sound.
With distance between us
I let out a sigh,
'Cause I'd sure hate to have
To kiss her goodbye.
The very next morning
After I was wed,
I let out a scream
And jumped from the bed.
I began to shake
And weep like a willow,
For there was ugly all over
The very next pillow.
From that moment on
I vowed over and over
To refrain from drinking
And always stay sober.
If you think my wife's
Not as ugly as this seems,
When she looks in the mirror,
She even screams.

The very last straw...
I've just had enough...
'Cause only last week
She began chewing snuff.
I'm not really complaining.
There's one reason why.
It's just that she's married
To this perfect guy.
So men take my warnings
As I tell you goodbye.
I'm not signing my name,
Just "Mr. Nice Guy."

Bill and Will

Here are two little words
Just so you can see
How frustrating and confusing
Our English can be.

I have a friend Wilbur,
But he goes by WILL.
Another named William
Who they all call BILL.

When you're a bit stubborn,
You have a strong WILL.
If you're buying on credit,
Well, you'll get a BILL.

Before leaving this Earth
We should all have a WILL.
See that cute little duck
With a long yellow BILL?

"I think this WILL work!"
Sometimes we WILL say.
They just passed a BILL
In the congress today.

The BILL on my cap
Protects me from the sun.
To keep these words straight
Sometimes is not fun.

It's probably as difficult
As any language can be.
And the one most confused,
Well, I'm sure that it's me.

Is the Sky Blue?

"What color is the sky?" I ask.
Why, of course, the sky is blue.
But what about the grays and black,
When a storm begins to brew
And when the sun is going down,
There's red, and orange, and pink.
To answer that the sky is blue.
Is silly don't you think?

About the Cover

I was frantic. I had all but finished my book, but no cover. I had ideas coming from everywhere, and had asked our friend Chip in western Kansas to design the cover for me. He came up with a beautiful dried rose picture, but that just wasn't what I had in mind. Then on July 21 everything just fell into place like a puzzle. I opened a drawer in my spare bedroom and there it was. I found an 1880 sewing machine instruction book full of pictures. The one on my cover is one of them, and the background came from the back cover of that same book. The rest of my art work came in the mail, and what I thought would never happen all came together.

About the Author

Sandra Parr Stonecipher was born in 1940 on a farm a few miles outside the small village of Summum, Illinois. When she was 5, the family moved to Summum, where she grew up. This is her first collection of poetry. She lives in Wichita, Kansas, with husband Marion "Stoney" Stonecipher.

To order additional copies of Threads of Life, complete the information below.

Ship to: (please print)

Name _____

Address_____

City, State, Zip_____

Day Phone_____

     Copies of Threads of Life @ 11.95 Each $_____

     Postage and handling @ 1.00 per book $_____

     Total amount enclosed $ _____

     Makes checks payable to: Sandra Stonecipher

     Send to: Sandra Stonecipher

     323 No. Knight Street

     Wichita, KS. 67203

     Order by E-mail: summum@sbcglobal.net

To order additional copies of Threads of Life, complete the information below.

Ship to: (please print)

Name _____

Address_____

City, State, Zip_____

Day Phone_____

     Copies of Threads of Life @ 11.95 Each $_____

     Postage and handling @ 1.00 per book $_____

     Total amount enclosed $ _____

     Makes checks payable to: Sandra Stonecipher

     Send to: Sandra Stonecipher

     323 No. Knight Street

     Wichita, KS. 67203

     Order by E-mail: summum@sbcglobal.net